## Hey Swim Buddies 👋

Congratulations!! Your comprehensive toolkit for effective and engaging swimming lessons has just arrived.

Inside, you'll find 150 vibrant swim cue cards designed to create visual prompts, timetables and schedules for your swimming classes.

Each card is a powerful tool to enhance communication and understanding, for swimmers of all abilities.

Whether you're a seasoned swim instructor or a parent looking to support your child's aquatic journey, these visual aids are your partners in progress.

Let's empower swimmers of all abilities, equip swim instructors with the tools they need, and support neurodiverse learners on their path to swimming success.

Together, we can create a more inclusive and welcoming swimming community for everyone.

Sharing swimming awesomeness,

*Alyt*

By the way...if you love this book blow up the comments & give us some ★★★★★
Stay in the loop! Follow us on your favourite socials!

   E

Insta @learntoswimtheaustralianway  Etsy www.borntoswimglobal.etsy.com  Facebook @swimmechanics

Be sure to drop us a 'like' or 'tag us' on socials if you find our stuff helpful

www.BornToSwim.com.au

# Visual Aids For Inclusive Aquatic Education
## By Allison Tyson

Written by AlyT
Copyright 2024 by Allison Tyson. All rights reserved.

First printing: May, 2024

Disclaimer
While we draw on our professional expertise and background in teaching learn to swim and swimming training, by purchasing and reading our products you acknowledge that we have produced this book for informational and educational purposes only. You alone are solely responsible and take full responsibility for your own wellbeing as well as the health, lives and well-being of your family and children in your care in and around water.

Stay in touch:
Born to Swim, P.O Box 6699, Cairns City, QLD 4870
SwimMechanics@yahoo.com
www.BornToSwim.com.au
www.PoweredByChlorine.com
Instagram @LearnToSwimTheAustralianWay
Etsy Store www.borntoswimglobal.etsy.com
Most titles available from Etsy, Amazon and all good online Book Retailers

Other titles by this Author:
Water Awareness Newborns
Water Awareness Babies
Water Awareness Toddlers
Learn to Swim the Australian Way Level 1 The Foundations
Learn to Swim the Australian Way Level 2 The Basics
Learn to Swim the Australian Way Level 3 Intermediate
Learn to Swim the Australian Way Level 4 Advanced
The Ultimate Pool Party Planner
Focus On Freestyle: Teaching Guide
Water Safety: Teaching Guide
Breaststroke Bootcamp: Teaching Guide
Butterfly Bootcamp: Teaching Guide
Backstroke Bootcamp: Teaching Guide
Learning To Float: Color Me In & Learn To Swim Activity Book
A Float For Every Stroke: Teaching Body Position
Visual Aids For Inclusive Aquatic Education: 100+ Swimming Flashcards
Welcome To Swim Squad: Activity Book For Swimmers
Welcome To Water Safety: Activity Book For Swimmers
Eat Pray Swim: A Swimmer's Logbook & Prayer Journal
Thalassophile: Logbook & Journal For Lovers Of The Ocean and Sea
Competitive Swimming Quotes: Coloring Pages For Big Kids, Teens & Tweens
Wild Swimming Quotes: Coloring Pages For Big Kids, Teens & Tweens
Mermaids: Coloring Pages For Big Kids, Teens & Tweens
Powered By Chlorine : Logbooks & Journals For Swimmers
17 Fun Floats: Creative Swim Poses For Confident Kids

# How To Use This Booklet

1. Grab your copy     2. Cut out the cue cards     3. Personalize them if you wish

3. Laminate for durability     4. Take them to the pool

Now you're ready to teach with confidence, knowing you have the support to reach every swimmer.

You can also create your own swimming schedules and tailor your teaching approach to meet the unique needs of each individual.

# learn to swim visuals

# close your mouth

# hold your breath

# put your face under

# wet your ears

# float with the kickboard

# hold onto the side

# look at your feet

# bend your knees

# torpedo stretch

# torpedo arms

# crouch down

# push off

# jump in

# bob up and down

# float

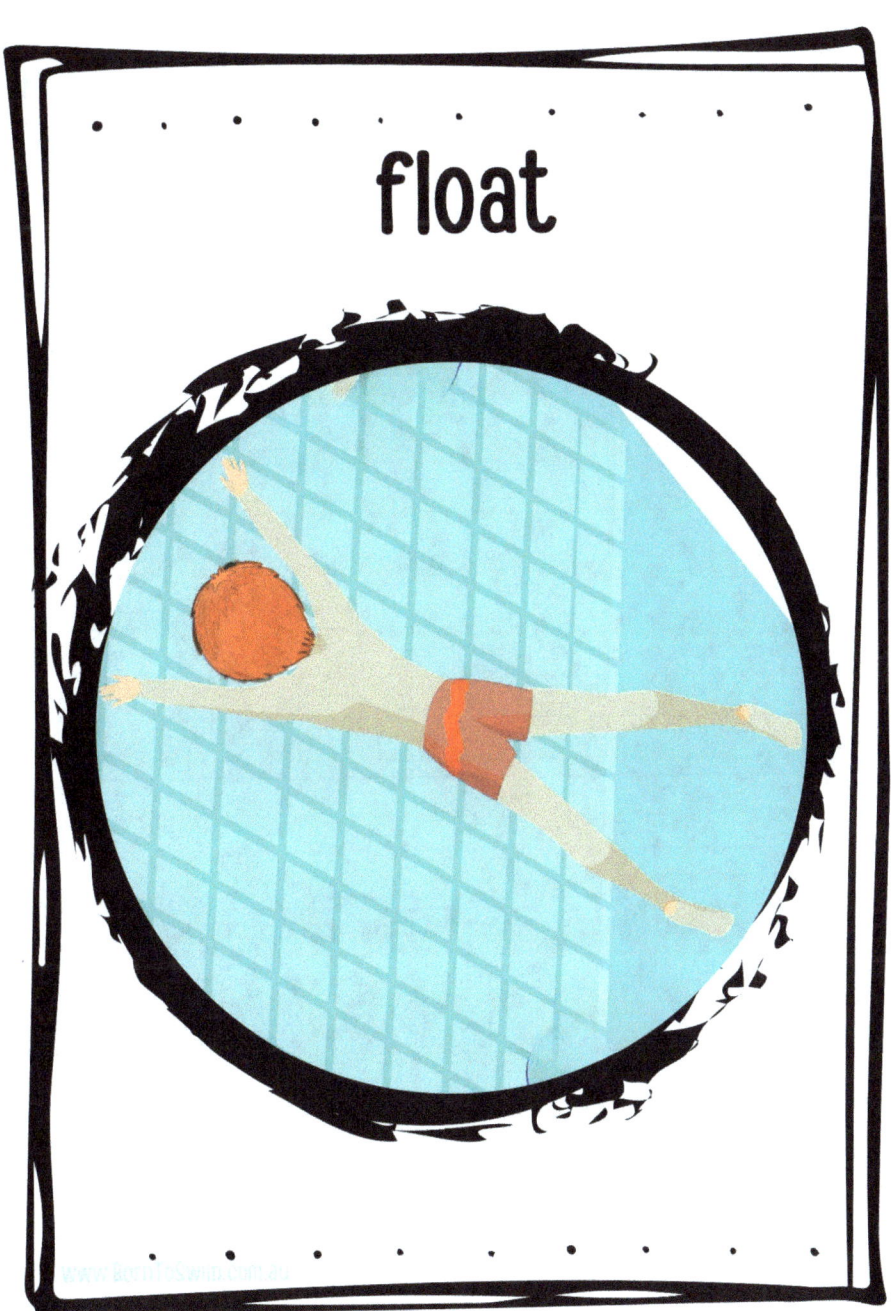

# kickboard float

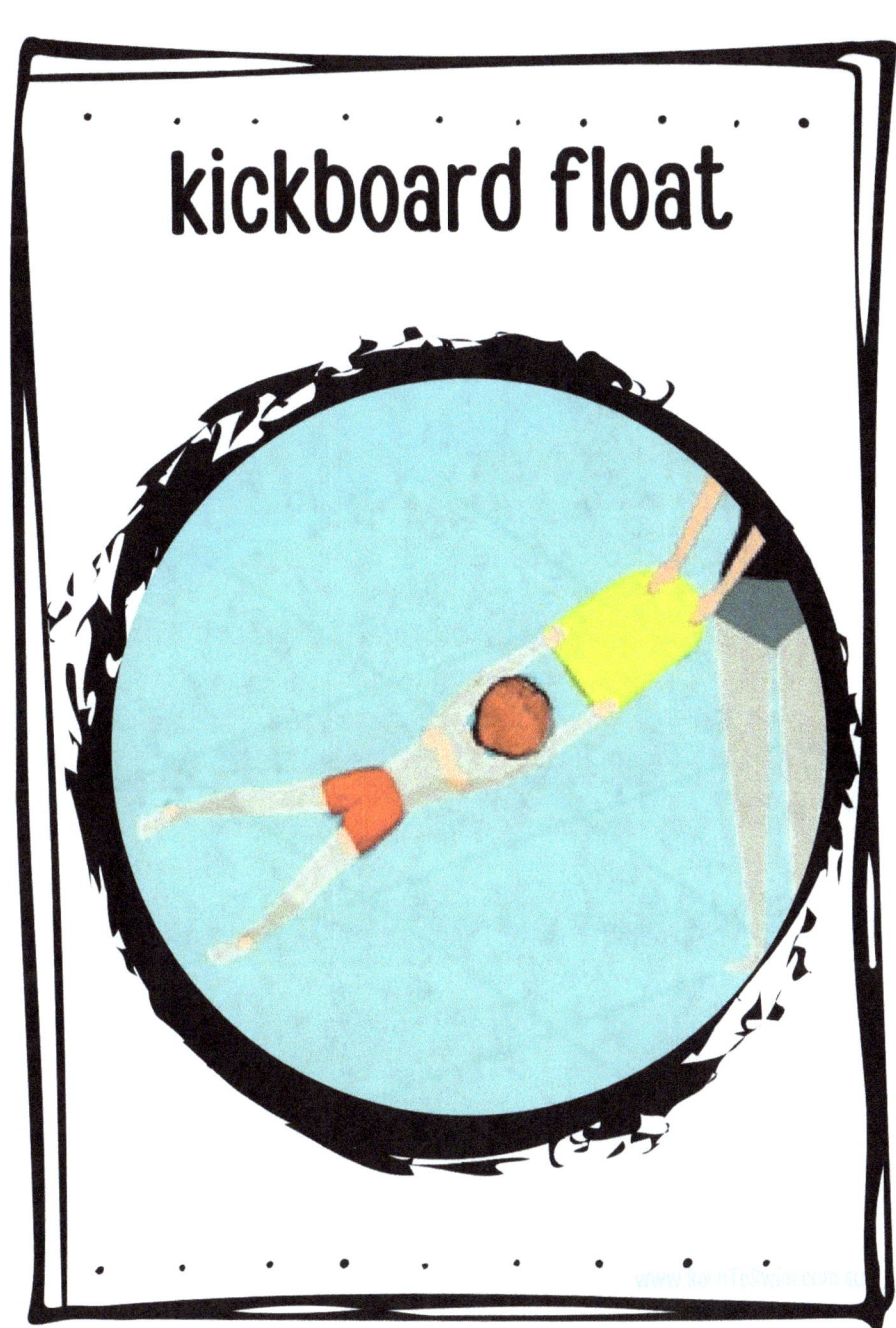

# float

# monkey-monkey

# climb out

# sit on the edge

# reach and paddle

# kick

# blow bubbles

# heels together

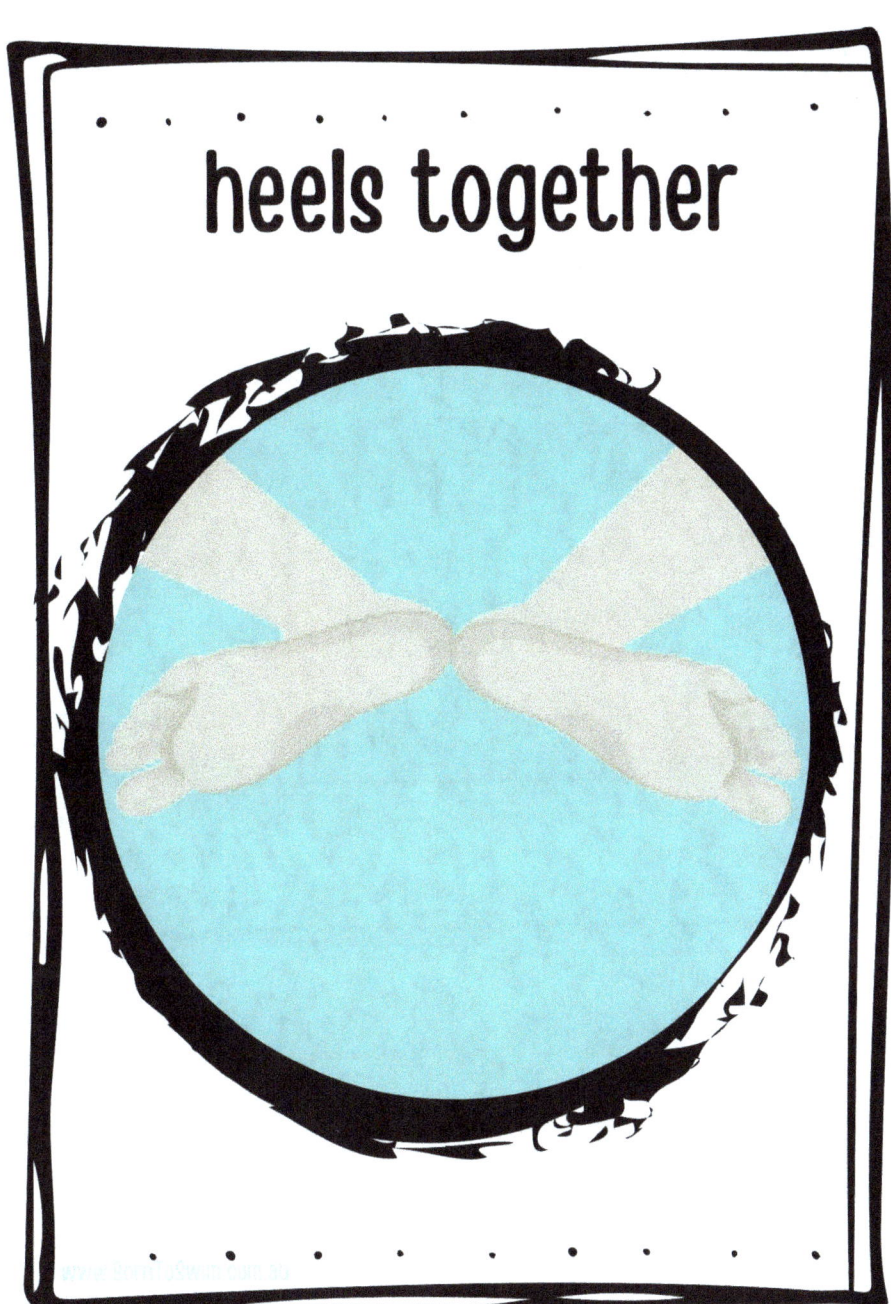

# Spin

# kick

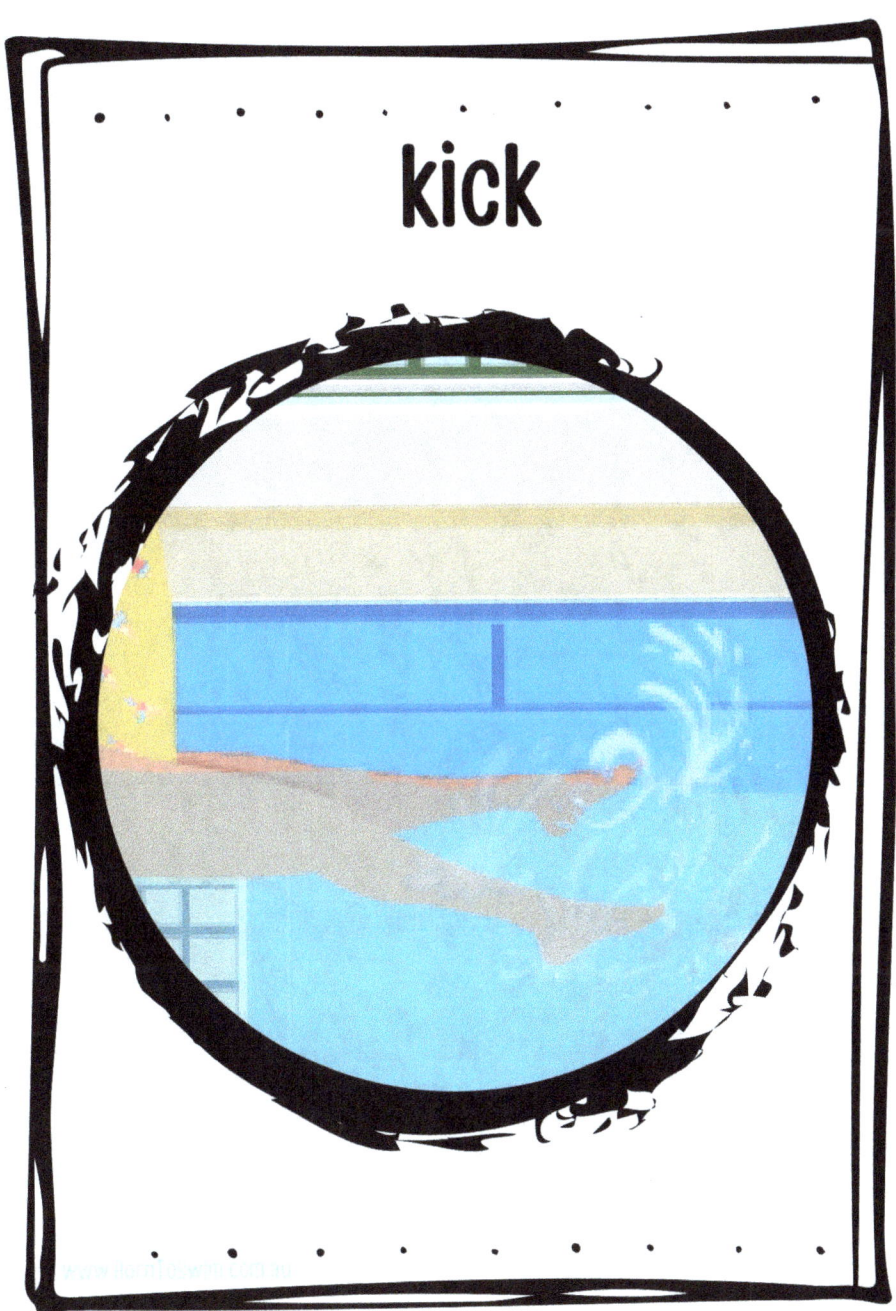

# survival backstroke

# kick on your back

# kick on your front

# seated dive

# frog float

# hold onto the wall

# backstroke

# head back ears under

# jump in

# stride entry

# dolphin kick

# tumble

# breaststroke arms

# hold the noodle

# butterfly pull

# backstroke push

# breastroke pull

# swim with the kickboard

# signal for help

# face in the water

# breathe to the side

# kickboard float

# side stroke

# freestyle

# breaststroke kick

# push out

# hyperstreamline

# breaststroke

# backstroke start

# butterfly

# swimming race

# reach rescue

# fun floats

# aeroplane float

# soldier float

# missile float

# mushroom float

# pencil float

# swimming

# directives

# listen

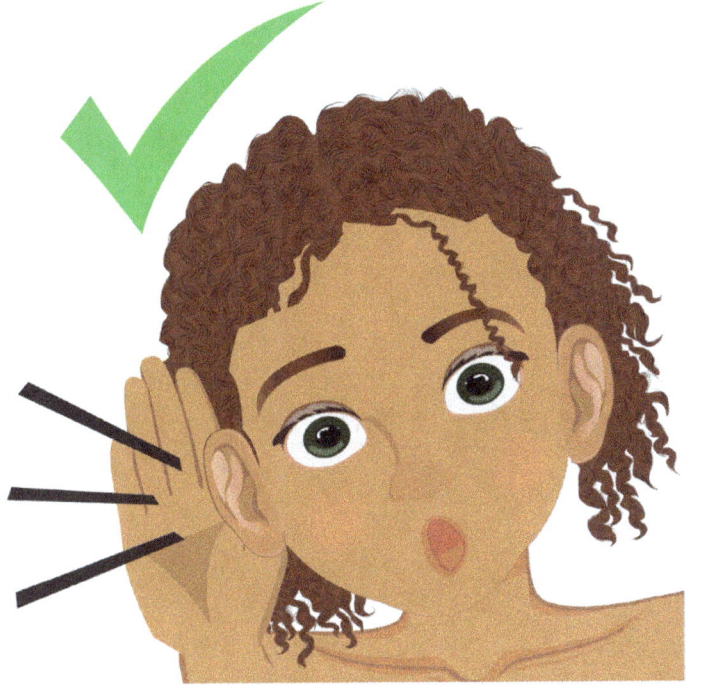

# watch

stop

# water safety

danger

**DANGER**

# bathrooms

# stay upright

# goggles on

# swimming cap

# swimming gear visuals

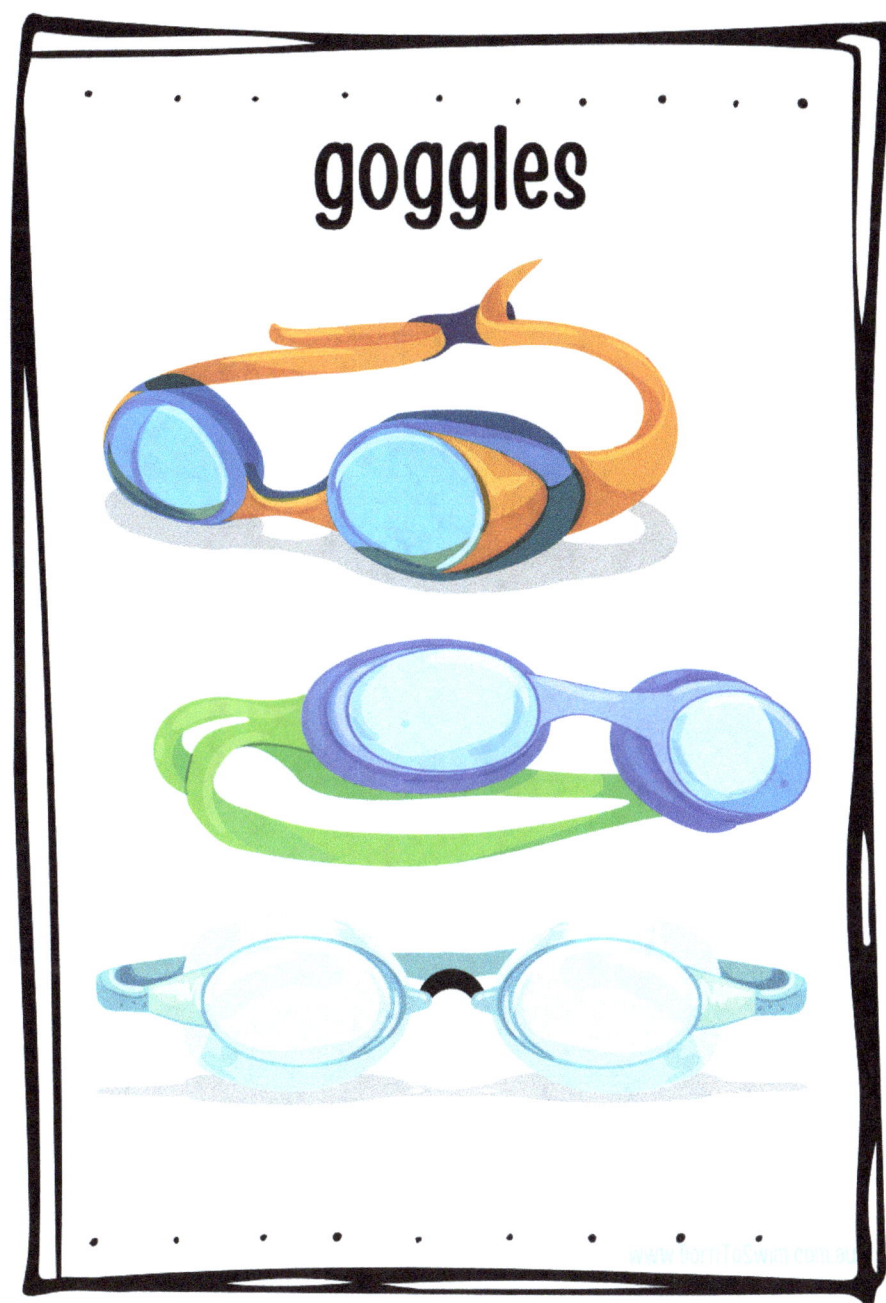

# towel

# kickboard

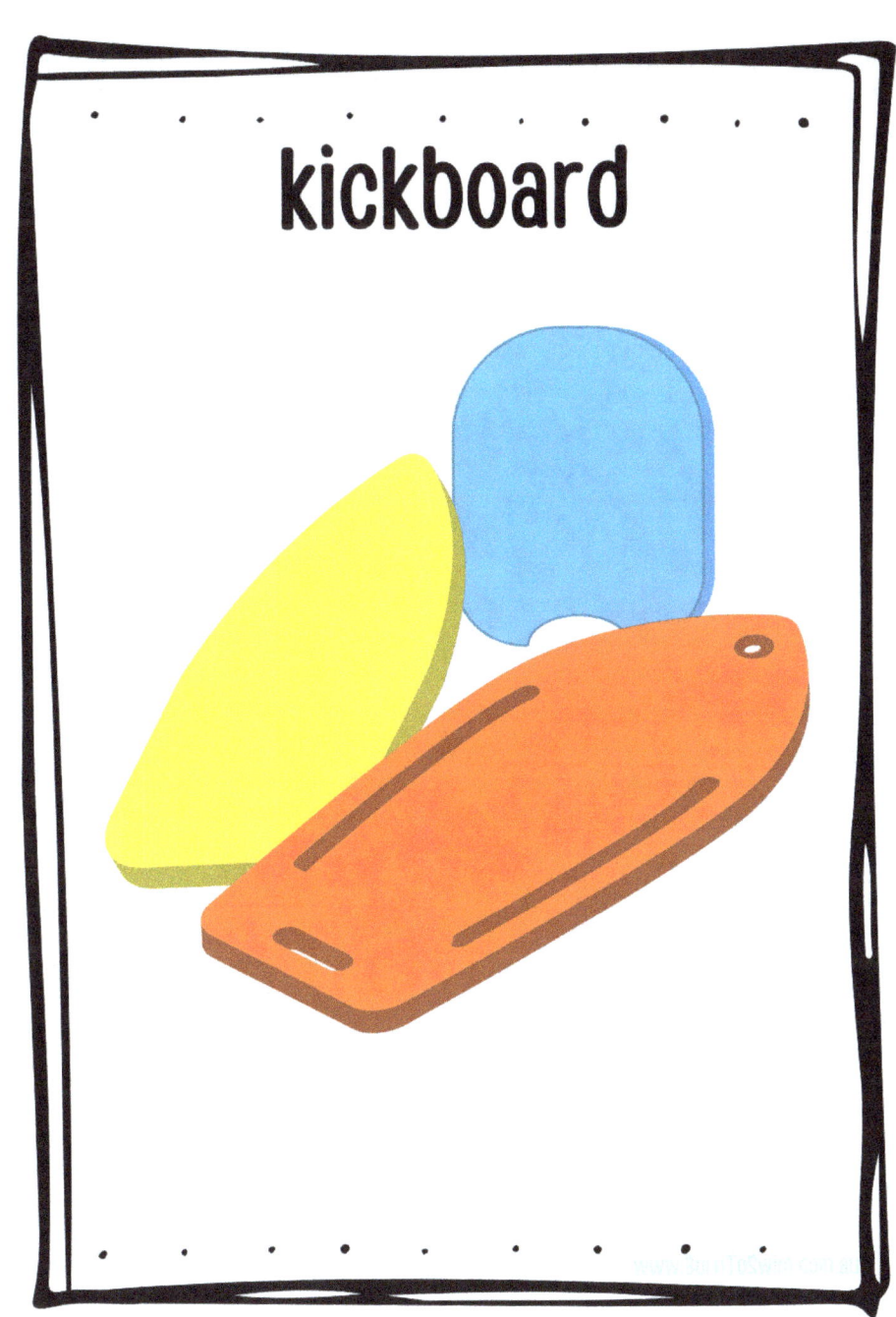

# ball

# umbrella

# swimwear

# flippers

# pool shoes

# pool floats

# drink bottle

# pool noodles

# swim bag

# whistle

# lifebuoy ring

# lifeguard

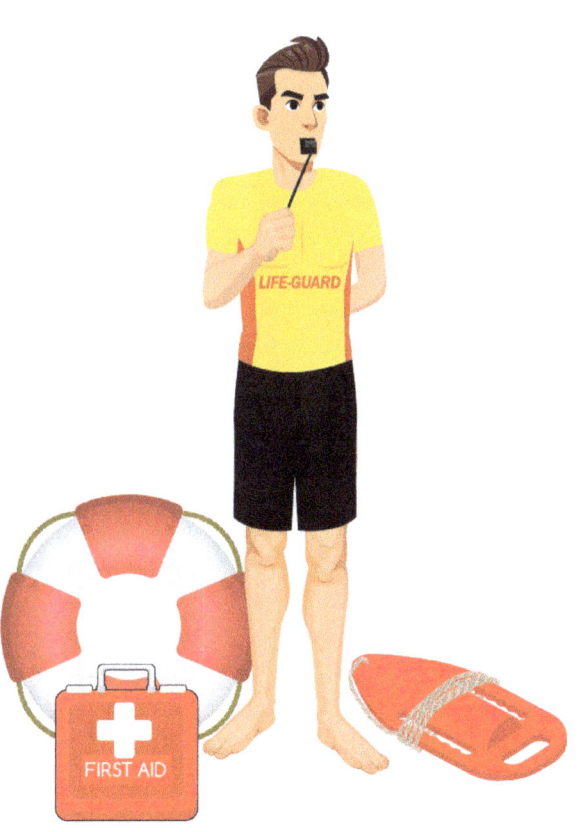

# lane ropes

# pull buoy

# water based activities

# pool

# water slide

# lake

# canoeing

# sailing

# surfing

# fishing

# beach

# snorkeling

# swimming schedule visuals

# put on your swim suit

# put on sunscreen

# go to the bathroom

# dry off

# dry your hair

# put on your hat

Thanks for diving into 'Visual Aids For Inclusive Aquatic Education'!
We hope you had a splashingly good time exploring the world of swimming with our visual cue cards.

Stay in the swim of things by following us on Instagram @learntoswimtheaustralianway for more swimming tips, updates, and fun content.

Keep swimming, keep learning, and keep making waves in the world of swimming education!
If you're hungry for more aquatic adventures, don't forget to check out our other books from the Learn To Swim The Australian Way Series on our website www.borntoswim.com.au
There's a sea of knowledge waiting for you!

www.ingramcontent.com/pod-product-compliance
Lightning Source LLC
Chambersburg PA
CBHW051419290426
44109CB00016B/1361